Laughter
Brought Me Out

Debra A. Decembly

© Copyright 2022

IBG Publications, Inc.

Published by I.B.G. Publications, LLC, a Power to Wealth Company
Web Address: WWW.IBGPublications.Com
admin@IBGPublications.Com / 904-419-9810
Copyright, 2022 by Debra A. Decembly
IBG Publications, LLC, Jacksonville, FL
ISBN: 978-1-956266-33-7

Decembly, Debra A.
Laughter Brought Me Out
WWW.DebraDecembly.Com

Unless otherwise noted, all scriptures are taken from the King James Version of the Bible.

Printed in the United States of America.

⁓Dedication

This book is dedicated to my parents:

My Father, the late 'Perry G. Decembly' & my mother, Mrs. Eva Mae Decembly.

Thank you for allowing me to be who God called me to be.

TABLE OF CONTENTS

Acknowledgments

I want to first acknowledge those who were instrumental in me writing this book. There were so many who I owe so much gratitude for my spiritual growth and the person who I am today.

Special Thanks go to the late Pastor Henry Clinkscale, Pastor Philip and Sylvia Iner, Pastor Will and Rose Parker, Sr., The late Apostle Loretta, J. Pernice, the late Apostle Moses Mason, Joan Mason, and the late Joe C. Coleman.

Thank you all!

Laughter Brought Me Out

Chapter 1

My Humble Beginnings

For you formed my inward parts; you knitted me together in my mother's womb. I praise you, for I am fearfully and wonderfully made. Wonderful are your works; my soul knows it very well. My frame was not hidden from you, when I was being made in secret, intricately woven in the depths of the earth. Your eyes saw my unformed substance; in your book were written, every one of them, the days that were formed for me, when as yet there was none of them.

~Psalm 139:1-16 (ESV)

It all started fifty three years ago on June 3, 1955, at Northside Hospital in Youngstown, Ohio. I was the first child of my father who had two other stepchildren with my mother.

Even as a child, as I was growing up, I've always had a curiosity with nature, and I desired to experiece it's beauty. Some would say I was nosy.

I can remember at the tender age of five living in the attic at my aunt's house. I would hear unknown sounds coming from the back of the attic where my parents were sleeping. This aroused my curiosity even more, and I remember peeping around the sheets.

There were sheets that separated the rooms where I attempted to see what was going on. That's when I came to realize that some things are not a child's business. But it seemed like adults' business was so interesting to me.

On this particular day, as I was doing my regular peeping. This was the day my father was coming out, and he accidentally ran into me with a cup of coffee in his hands.

What a disaster!

It would have been. I escaped getting burned. During this time in my life, we were living there with two other sets of families. This included my mother, and my two younger sisters.

It was a house full of people and we all walked to school together: cousins, five boys and two girls. We would play together and fight one another; but we still love one another even to this day.

The Times When I Grew Up

The era I grew up in, children were taught to be seen and not heard. This was not necessarily a good thing if you really think about it. Children desire to tell parents things they were not ready to hear. For example, a child may need to tell their parents that someone is touching them inappropriately.

I was afraid to go to sleep because I did not know who was going to get into bed with me. Being told to be 'seen and not heard' caused me to suppress these awful, hurtful things deep inside. At some point, you forget that these feelings are there, not realizing you are as sick as your secret.

Everything was hush, hush, taboo. Keep quiet. What happens in this house stays in this house. And don't you dare speak of these things.

I can remember that one of my oldest cousins, who was a few years older than me had a bicycle. The bycycle was too big for me and my legs could barely reach the pedals. The bike had a bar across the front, which means that it was a boy's bicycle.

One day, I was being mischievious and decided that I was going to ride it. I came out of my auntie's house, climbed on the third step and struggled to put my short legs over the bar. At five years old, I was unable to get my feet to reach the pedals. Into the street, me and the bike went, and I ran right into the side of a parked car. I fell, and one of my cousin's ran into the house to tell my parents what happened.

Boy was I in trouble for more than one reason. The main reason was because I should have not been on the bike in the first place, I could have been seriously hurt. For all those reasons, I received a good old fashioned spanking.

The Blessing Of My Auntie's House

First and foremost, living with my auntie was a blessing. Every day, all of the children sat down as a family for breakfast and dinner.

Her home was always full of people all the time. It was us, but I had an older sister who had some challenges that interfered with her daily living. One of her challenges was that she would stutter whenever she spoke, made funny noises and jumped around, walking on her tip toes.

It seemed to me that the majority of the time she received a lot of attention. I liked helping her and taking care of all my sisters. It gave me a sense of importance.

There were times when Lynn would fight us. I believe she did that because she knew we didn't understand her and it frustrated her. This was how she communicated her frustrations. At times, she would be rough, but in reality she didn't mean it.

I knew as a little girl that she needed my help, and I wanted to help her. So, our positions changed. I stepped into being the bigger sister, even though she was a handful at times. I made sure she felt loved and secure.

Many times her speech was choppy, and not fluent at all. She could say a few words. Since we were close in age, she surprised me by learning how to say, 'Debbie.'

I knew that I had a great responsibility in the house due to safety. But now we can say due to her 'disabilities.' This was in the early sixties when words such as 'mental illness' were not spoken; especially for black men.

* * *

My father and a lot of other black men were laid off frequently, and we didn't have much to eat or nice clothes to wear. One thing for certain, and another thing for sure, we had both our parents in the home and that meant a lot to me.

Dad worked while mom stayed home taking care of the house and her children. There were times she went out and cleaned houses and ironed clothes. That was what a lot of black women did during those times. They did not have full time jobs, but worked long hours to earn small paychecks that hardly met the family's needs.

My Early Days In School...

It was right before I started kindergarten when we moved into our first home. As a child, I believed this house was so nice. We had an upstairs, basement, and three bedrooms. In our backyard, there were apple and peach trees.

I was in heaven even though the house was not full like my auntie's house. My dad believed in education and made sure that I went to school. He decided to get me started in school at the tender age of four and a half years old. This is when I learned my colors, how to write my name, and count from one to fifty.

Learning was exciting to me!

Going to school made me feel like I was a big girl. When I went, I was happy growing up in an era when prayer was instituted in school.

When we first got to school in the morning, the whole classroom would stand up, bow their heads and have a silent prayer. We would also recite the Pledge of Allegiance. Now I was on to something new and unique to me because prayer gave me hope. It gave me a feeling deep down inside that I truly I can't explain.

My father prepared me at home for school and helped me when I went for the first time. While the teacher was teaching us sounds, I'd eagerly raise my hand, and answer quickly because my father had taught me at home.

Once my teacher saw how advanced I was, she would not allow me respond. She wanted to give the other children a chance to answer. I used to think that she was being mean to me, but I was too young to understand.

One day in class we were doing our morning review of the sounds of the alphabets and immediately my hand went up. The teacher thought I was going to respond to the question, but the truth was, I had to go to the restroom. She never acknowledged my hand and I ended up making a mess in my clothes.

I was so ashamed.

Everyone was saying in the class that there was a smell. I knew the smell was me, so I couldn't wait to get home to take off my red and black tights. I ran all the way home and hid them next to a pile of dirty clothes.

My mother began to smell the awful smell. My clothes had been sitting so long that they became hard. Once my mother learned what happened, she asked me, "Why didn't you ask to use the restroom?"

I couldn't say, "I don't know," because I never knew why. I just said, "The teacher wouldn't let me."

We never discussed that conversation again.

The Times I Lived In...

Don't forget, we were in the sixties and there was prejudice at that time. I was too young to understand why my dad was constantly being laid off. By this time, we had lost our home, and as a child, this was so disturbing. I was attempting to figure out why we had to move again.

We had to go to a different school and learn how to make new friends. What I didn't realize was that God was preparing me for change at such an early age.

This time, we moved to a different neighborhood which was on the rundown side of town where rats and roaches invaded our home. We were renting the house and it seemed like there were roaches everywhere. A roach got in my ear and I had to go to the doctor. That day I made a vow that when I grew up and had a house, I'd never have rats or roaches.

By this time, I was in the second grade in the year of 1963. This was the same year that President John F. Kennedy was assassinated. I can still see the book on my teachers desk and the look on my teachers face: Ms. Susan Jones.

When she received the news from two of her colleagues, it seemed like everyone was crying. School was dismissed early to give everyone the space to grieve. I noticed that darkness swept the school and nothing was the same after that.

The same year, I had a hard time in school. It was especially hard to pronounce words with CH, SH, and ER in it. During this time, there was a speech class. After the administration staff communicated with my parents, speech class was recommended for me.

My second grade teacher, Mrs. Jones insisted I attend speech classes because she was disturbed by the way I talked at times. It made her so frustrated that I can remember Mrs. Jones giving us a test and she handed me a answer sheet with most of the answers already marked in pencil.

Here I am, a child and thinking this was not right. I raised my hand and told Mrs. Jones what I found. She never responded, so I continued taking the test ignoring the penciled answers.

When the test came back, Mrs. Jones was so upset with me she called me up to her desk and began nicely explaining to me that she was the one who marked the answer sheet for me. She went on to tell me that she would help me for the next two years.

Our Neighborhood

As a child, all I could think about is how we lived in that 'old ugly house.' Mom was always preparing meals for us whenever we had food.

At times, we were allowed to go play with the other children in the neighborhood. Back in those good old days, everyone knew the parents next door. If you did anything, and another parent saw you, by the time you got home your parents already knew.

Life at that time was just different. As children, we could play dodgeball in the street, as well as kickball. As girls, we played games, like hopscotch, jacks and coloring books.

If we got into a disagreement, even as best friends, we would fight it out and go back to being friends. There were no guns shooting at one another.

One day, my mother cooked spaghetti and it was so good that I wanted another helping. The problem with that was there was only enough left for my dad who wasn't home from work yet. Being a child, I did not understand. All I knew was that I wanted more.

While my mom's back was turned, I stuck my hand in the pot and ate more. Right away, my mother noticed a difference in the pot. As a child I wondered how she knew, but the evidence was all over my face.

Boy did I get a good old fashioned but spanking that day. My dad knew that I did not like spankings. But through this experience, I learned that anything I wanted, all I had to do was ask, even if the answer was 'no.'

I never noticed the other children in the neighborhood. They all seemed to dress better, looked neater and cleaner than us. They also had cars. So in my mind, I thought their families had to be better because of their appearance.

I learned so much having fun as a child. There were a lot of games that girls could play, that were so much fun. We had fun playing jacks, hopscotch, riding bikes, and playing hide and go see. I taught my daughter and grandaughter those same games years later, and they loved them.

On Sundays we'd sit down as a family and listen to the Rex Humbard show and other gospel singing groups on the radio.

It was so nice when we would sit together and listen to the radio. We'd be in front of the radio, and this was our family time together.

Unfortunately, we were not allowed to have playmates over to our house. I believe the reason was due to our living conditions. Being a child, I thought we were the only ones who were poor without nice furniture.I had no clue about the struggles my parents had to go through.

I loved going to school to get away from the house if for no other reason than to enjoy prayer. It was something about praying that excited me. My whole being would be so happy and rejoicing when we prayed. Words cannot explain how I felt. It gave me something I never had before: hope.

I grabbed hold to prayer and began exercising it daily. I can remember going to and from school, walking and talking to God about what was going on in my home. I watched my mother get up daily, frustrated, but handling her business as a wife and mother just like any other mother would.

A Family Separation...

All four girls were sleeping one night when Lynn got very upset. One of the younger sisters had an accident, and she was furious. Being upset, she fought her younger sister but did not understand that she sealed her own fate.

The next day, my mother did not see any harm in it and she sent me to school. During this time, the officials came to our door wanting to know what happened to May's face. Once it was explained, the authorities decided she could not stay there any longer.

The authories felt she couldn't defend herself as well as others and she was removed from the family in February of 1963. She needed twenty-four hour care with people who were trained and watchful and could determine an episode was coming.

This was a heartbreaking situation, but my parents had no choice but to let her go. When she left, it left a void in my life. I was lonely, depressed and angry because I did not truly understand why she had to leave us.

Why couldn't she stay?

My whole world fell from underneath me. She gave me purpose, responsibility and a sense of love. I knew she needed me and I needed her. For as long as I could remember, there was a sadness in our home for a very long time.

* * *

We had moved, and here we were again. We were starting another school, meeting new classmates, teachers and the whole ordeal. The area was different and so were the children. They were taller, rougher, meaner, and always ready to fight for no apparent reason. Some of these children's parents became my parents' associates when it came to drinking, partying, and playing Keno over one another's house.

Even though our parents interacted with one another, it did not change their behavior when it came to bullying us. The difference between us and them was their size. They were so much bigger than us. They looked like giants and we looked like ants.

There were times when we saw them, we'd take off running, and duck in the bushes to hide behind houses. We had to walk by ourelves.

My brother being a boy, did what boys did and would hang out with the boys. There was a school close to us, but we were on the borderline of not going to that school. It was a relief because that was the same school the bullies went to.

The school board said we had to go to the school that was ten blocks away, and that was just as bad. Either way we walked home, we always got chased being the new kids on the block. We were always attempting to find another way home.

There were times we lucked up, and no one would see us. Then there were times when they did. We were always running home daily, as well as to the corner store. We did not know as children that *other* children would fight us, but we found out.

Snooping Around In The Attic

I began hiding in the attic, and to my surprise, I found personal items belonging to my parents. It may have been wrong to go through someone's private things, but it was a good thing because you never know what you will find.

Strangely, I came upon my parents marriage license and I also found both of my sisters' birth certificates. To our amazement, we learned that we were celebrating the wrong dates for years.

My mother was not surprised at what we found. Being a little girl, I found her costume jewelry and I would wear it when she wasn't at home. As soon as I saw her coming up the driveway, I woulld run to put it back where I found it.

Our house was always filled with my with my brother's friends. Whenever my parents were not home, they would go drinking. My parents would be gone for a while.

He was always telling his friends to stay away from his sisters' rooms because they were constantly questioning him about us. They would ask, "What were our names? How old were we?" Once he warned them about us, they stopped talking to us.

McKinley had more freedom than the girls and he was never at home. He wanted to be a boy and do what boys did at his age. Watching his sisters were not his plans.

McKinley had more privileges than us, being the oldest and a boy. At times he was impatient, mean to us, and it seemed like we got on his nerves. My Mama used to say he was like his father.

On the street we lived, our house was in the middle between two other houses. We had a dirt front yard with no grass where we played most of the time.

My father wanted a son but he had five girls who seemed to enjoy spending quality time with him on the days he wasn't working or drinking. Because we did not have any toys, he would call us outside and show us so many games we could play. We'd play games like softball, kickball, and dodgeball. This taught us about good sportsmanship.

He would not allow us to get mad if we lost. There were times that I would catch him laughing at us, showing us it was only a game an nothing to get upset about. You can rest assure there was a sore loser in the bunch.

My father would always help us with our homework. He was very special, and made many sacrifices for his children. He took his fatherhood seriously and he always dropped nuggets to us. We all loved and adored my father, he was one in a million.

* * *

Our neighborhood had a lot of bootleg houses where our parents would go to drink and play cards. Sometimes they would go solo or together, which was not a good idea.

Maybe fourty five minutes later, one of them would come home alone and upset at the other. Majority of the time, mama would be upset with daddy, saying women would be flirting with him. Daddy did not notice, but mom wanted him to say something. He would never reply, because he was peaceful.

But what could he say? Surprisingly, he'd shrugg it off and walk away. Womanizing wasn't who he was at all. Alcohol makes you see things that really aren't there and it can play tricks on your eyesight.

When our parents were doing what they did, we would wonder around the neighborhood. As young, immature girls, we were not aware that it was not a good idea.

Back in those days, we could purchase cigarettes at the corner stores for our parents and they were only twenty eight cents per pack. Most of the time, myself and one of my sisters went to the store for cigarettes right before the store closed. We could walk up the street at 8:30 PM at night because times were different then and crime was not on the rise. The streets were a lot safer then.

Many people left their doors unlocked in the sixties, and everyone looked out for one another. If an adult saw you somewhere you were not supposed to be, by the time you got home, your parents knew it.

My mom had a saying, "You think you are getting away with something."

Most of the time, it took longer to get home because we had to pass a house with hedges. It was just something about that house, and I hated walking past it. We never knew who lived there.

Seemingly those rough, tall boys happened to be in the hedges. At times, they would jump out taking pleasure in scaring us. This made us dread going to that store.

We decided to walk in the street because it was easier than the sidewalk. We just wanted a headstart on those tall boys who terrorized us. We didn't know what they wanted with us and we didn't want to find out.

I detested them. As a matter of fact, I was afraid of them.

As we were walking, Rhonda who was a year younger than me saw them. I believe she had a crush on one of the boys because she would smile whenever they came around. She was hoping he would notice her, yet the girls in the neighborhood did not want to be anywhere near them.

Those unappealing neighborhood boys seem to know when my parents were not home. Out of nowhere they'd show up at our house. One thing for sure was McKinley would tell those boys that they needed to leave.

At that moment my feelings changed.

When I was around nine or ten years old, McKinley began touching me in appropriate places which I did not like. I told him that as my brother, we were not supposed to touch each other like that. It was not normal, and from that moment, I was determined that he was not going to touch me.

We were home alone on a particular Saturday, and my parents left to go drinking. McKinley decided he wanted to chase us around the house and we ended up in the basement, breaking a mirror.

Running back upstairs, I knew he was after me this day, because he followed me. The hallway had double doors and I hid behind the doors. I was so busy trying to hide that I wasn't looking carefully and I slammed my finger in between the doors. My little pinky finger got caught in the door.

When I took my hand out from between the doors, my nail on my pinky was gone. Even until this day, the nail doesn't grow, and my finger doesn't close with the rest of the fingers on my hand.

One of my uncles who was married to one of my mother's younger sisters came by looking for my parents. He saw my hand wrapped up in a towel bleeding, so he put me in his car, and took me to the hospital.

My aunt's husband stayed the whole time with me. I received stitches and my finger got wrapped up. I had to wear a special splinter on that finger for nearly a year and had to learn to write with my left hand; this was extremely hard. I never told anyone what happened, especially my parents.

God began performing a work in my life.

* * *

At the age of fourty seven, I finally told my mother after all those years what happened to my finger. She was so shocked when I told her about my brother. To my surprise, she said, "Debbie I never knew and I'm so sorry."

* * *

Momma did not know

But at that moment, I became free from the shackles that had been holding me since I was about nine years old.

If the Son therefore shall make you free, ye shall be free indeed.
~John 8:36 (KJV)

I was not sure if she believed me or not. So she asked Rhonda about everything that I said. Rhonda told our mother it was true. Even though Rhonda confirmed what I said was true, she wanted to know what made me tell her. I told my sister I needed to be free. Nevertheless it was my truth.

We were taught, 'what happened in the house stayed in the house.' These became our family's secrets. But after that incident, McKinley left me alone.

* * *

One of my brother's friends who lived across the street began noticing me. The problem with this is that I did not love myself. Sometimes you can be engaged with someone and it won't not mean you any good.

He would call me over to his house when I was walking to the store, pretending to ask about McKinley. All of a sudden the conversations switched to me, and the next thing I knew, I was inside his house. Before I knew it, I was on the couch and it happened so quickly; we had sex.

Just like that.

This continued every time I went to the store. He was a little older, and I didn't like him at all. After a while, I decided to stop giving him what he wanted whenever he saw me. I told him 'no' and I meant it. I just didn't know why.

He cornered me one day and asked me 'why?' I told him because I did not want to have sex anymore.

Introduced To Church

My mom and dad were not church people at all. Here we were, four little girls who didn't know a thing about church etiquette, or how protocol went. When we saw people shouting, out of ignorance, we would laugh and be so unruly in God's house. People constantly told us to be quiet, but we were so disruptive and continued doing it every week. Our parents were doing the best they could, yet this was the result of children left unattended.

At Easter time, we'd be so pretty with all those ribbons in our straightened hair, black patent leather shoes, and stockings. When we recited our Easter speeches, this was when our parents came to church. We practiced our speeches at home, so you can imagine how clear we sounded. When I grew up got older, I wanted to be noticed and heard, but I did not have the slightest idea how to go about it.

Being in the Lord's house made a huge difference in my life. Every time I went through something or a situation arose at home, I would go to the Lord's house.

My mother's oldest brother Lewis had a wife and she would straighten and curl my hair. I looked so pretty.

After church was over, I'd go back and play with my cousins, then go home. Sometimes I wished I could stay longer, but I knew I could not. I just never knew what I would face when I got home. Since I didn't get out the house much, I dreaded going home and wanted to enjoy every moment.

At the time, a lot was going on in our home. McKinley came and went as he pleased, and Rhonda had reached puberty, becoming defiant at times. She felt like she could do whatever she wanted.

Here she was, a teenager, and she would leave whenever she felt like it. She began staying out so much, my mother got worried. Of course she would be concerned about her daughter who was somewhere and she didn't know where.

At times, mother would call people to find out where Rhonda was. The stress in our home, the hurt, disappointment and disengagement made me want to be different from Rhonda.

So I threw myself into my schoolwork aspiring to be the best so my parents could be proud of me; I wanted to earn their trust. But I realized, no matter what I did, that feeling would not leave until Ronda was safe at home.

Although I sought the approval of my mom, she looked over me. Rhonda was getting away with a lot from my mother, and my dad tried to gain control of the situation, but he could not.

My Growth Process

I was now in the eighth grade, and during this time, my dad was working steady enough to catch up on the bills.

I became involved in track, running the 440 relay. I was great at track and field, but I also loved Home Economics class.

When my children were growing up, this class was not available. When I learned to sew, I began making wearing the clothes I made. But there were some projects I could not complete because I did not have a sewing machine at home.

I was dissapointed because I was not able to pursue something I loved.

When you're sad or disapointed, the devil knows how to set you up for a trap.

---

* * *

It was about this time that I noticed the mailman, and began having a conversation with him. I started smiling at him whenever he would bring the mail. He asked me how was school, I would tell him my problems, and he would listen.

When you are young, you are so impressionable. I developed an infatuation for him and began looking forward to him coming everyday. I fell so in love with him that I even knew when he was coming. It was like clockwork.

I'd be looking cute.

My mother noticed me eager to get to the mail, and one day made a comment saying, "Why are you always in his face smiling? He's older and possibly married."

My mother did not understand that he was so easy to talk to. He saw me, encouraged me, and listened to me. He was so understanding, and I could share all of my dreams with him. He was never out of line at any time.

Then something happened. Our conversations got longer and longer. Of course, like any good mother, she commented again and said, "I believe you are in love. Or you have a huge crush on him."

I denied it.

Then one day, he asked me if I had a boyfriend. I told him, 'no,' and all of my school girlfriends were going on dates to the skating rink, but I couldn't go.

Sometimes mothers remember when they were teenagers and assume that all girls are the same. My mother had so many girls and she was very protective of us, all the time. We thought she was mean, uncaring, and insensitive to us. But she really wasn't.

But what do you know when you are a teenager? Nothing. You don't understand how your parents felt until you become a mother yourself.

My Rebellion..

I remember there was a sock hop after school from 4:00-6:00 PM. That's what they called the dances at our school gym. I knew my mother was going to say no, so I said to myself, "I'm going to ask her anyway."

Sure enough, she did, she said no. I knew she would say 'no,' not even, 'allow me to think about it.'

But no.

On that day, I intentionally stayed over after school. I had a quarter, so I went to the sock hop despite what my mother said. For the first time in a long time, I was having so much fun. Time got away from me and I honestly did not mean to stay long.

At that point, I was afraid to go home since it was dark; so I didn't go. It was not as if something was wrong, I did not want to be disciplined. I was afraid to face not only my mother but my dad, who I did not want to disappoint.

Fear gripped me deep inside of my stomach. I had a school friend who lived just one block away from or house. She was also married and expecting a baby.

I went to her house not considering how worried my parents would be. They were already dealing with Rhonda and her behavior with skipping school. Now, here I am adding more sorrow than they needed.

Being away from home was no fun and it's not the same. I don't care what anyone says: There is no place like home!! Your family is at home.

Boy, was I blind and stupid! You can't do what you want in someone else's house. No way.

My parents taught me that no matter what, call home. Not only did I not return home, I had the nerve to stay away a couple of days. I called myself running away for something that I did.

I finally called home and one of my sisters answered and said "Debra, where are you?"

All I could say was, "I'm close by, not far."

I was homesick and I missed my family. Where I was staying temporarily, I saw a family unit which reminded me of my family. Oh how I missed my family; they were still my family, and there is no such thing as a perfect family.

By this time, I muscled up some strength, decided to face the music and go home. I had been gone two days and my parents had contacted the police. People were looking for me, and for the life of me, I could not understand why my mother thought I was with the mailman. I knew where I was, and I communicated.

My mother called the mailman's place of employment, requesting they put him on another route, and he was moved quickly. I found out all of this when I returned home. I told my mother, he was just a friend and nothing else. I later found out he was married with a son.

She felt like how we communicated was inappropriate; and it was. But my friend was gone and I was never going to see him again. He kept me laughing and smiling and became my saving grace so to speak.

I enjoyed laughing due to all I had been through. But my laughter had a lot of pain. Laughter was like medicine. It brought healing and made me feel good inside.

Laughter also brings a release.

A merry heart doeth good like a medicine: but a broken spirit drieth the bones..
~**Proverbs 17:22 (KJV)**

Here I was again, adjusting to another small loss. First my

sister, now a friend, then moving out of my aunt's house, to my sister being taken away.

How do you get used to loss? Feeling so abandoned?

The Loss Of Dr. Martin Luther King, Jr.

In addition to the losses I experienced that year, the black community suffered the loss of a very powerful Negro leader: Dr. Martin Luther King, Jr. He was assassinated.

April 4, 1968 was a very tragic, crucial time in the world for everyone. Dr. Martin Luther King, Jr. was a powerful voice for blacks during this era. He was a peaceful man who stood against injustice, and rallied for fairness and equality. When he was killed, everyone, especially the black community felt it.

Everyone was devastated to no end. The only way they could react was through violence, even though he preached and taught against it. He lived a life of 'no violence,' but the blacks were not hearing it. They closed their ears and reacted, despite what he demonstrated through his life.

I remember that day as if it were yesterday. When we got the news, I was in school. School was dismissed and everyone was told to go straight home.

People started rioting, looting, breaking in stores, and killing across the nation. Their pain was tremendous and there was an uproar. People were angry and hurt and other races had to be careful not to upset them at the time. America was saddened by his death and it shook the nation to no end.

At school, whites were being humiliated. I had some white friends, and I was afraid for them. I showed them shortcuts home to avoid the angry mobs. I didn't believe in violence, I am a peaceful person. I knew that race was the initial cause of what was going on, and it was greater than I could ever imagine.

When school was out, the national guard came in and we had a curfew. The newspaper at that time was full of so many events and a lot of it, I didn't fully understand. But my parents and other blacks viewed it a lot differently. Here was this black man, Dr. Martin Luther King, Jr. who blacks saw as a way out, or freedom.

A different movement came through this era, including the Black Panther Party. Positive messages circulated like, 'I'm black and I'm proud,' green, black and red, etc. This was the era when the Godfather of soul James Brown came out with the song, "I'm black and I'm proud."

The Vietnam War was still raging and it had a devastating effect on many of the brothers when they returned home. They witnessed so many deaths, and it changed their life mentally and emotionally.

My Developmental Years

During the next couple of years, I became a spelling champion in my home town for my home room. The home room was the first step after you compete with other winners on stage in the school auditorium. Then a spelling test came again.

Whenever I stood in front of people, I choked up. I would get stage fright or fear, and I wasn't sure how it gripped me. When they asked me to spell the word, I paralyzed.

When I saw their faces, the words would not come up. It came out wrong and the same thing happened the following year.

* * *

Running track was good for me, and it helped me with my frustrations. Practice was every day after school and lasted for an hour.

Although I enjoyed sports, being in junior high was entirely different from grade school. I was growing up and had to take gym classes. In order to participate in gym, you had to buy a gym uniform.

As soon as I found out, I told my parents and let them know there was a deadline to place the order with the gym instructor. Unfortunately we did not have the money and I missed the deadline.

My family and a few other girls didn't have the money for the uniform. We were given an alternative assignment and had to write whatever the gym teacher said, then hand it in at the end of the class.

The gym instructor was tough! Ms. Carla had been a sergeant in the Army, so she made us work until we saw results. The way she trained me, my body began to take shape, and boys noticed me like never before; I noticed them as well.

There was a dark skinned young school boy named Rodney King and we had the same classes together. I saw him looking at me one day in class smiling. We looked up from our papers and our eyes locked, smiling.

But that day, Rodney asked me if he could walk me home. Why not? I said, 'yes.' As we began to stroll along, we started talking and laughing just like young teenagers who have a crush on one another.

We talked about our family, school and whatever came to our minds. Then we ended up in front of my house on the sidewalk. Out of nowhere, he tried to plant a kiss on my lips. I felt like he was moving too soon and I said, 'No' politely. He tried again, and I said, 'No' again.

All of a sudden, his demeanor changed. All of the kindness he displayed was gone, and he got angry. He stepped back and slapped me so fast that I literally saw stars before my eyes. You know what I'm talking about?

Have you ever watched a cartoon character run into a tree, or a brick wall, their eyes cross, and stars appear over their head?

That is exactly how I felt.

That's how hard his slap was. We struggled for a brief moment but I was too stunned to cry at the moment because of the way I felt for him. I had an angry and hurt feeling.

He left me standing there, then he went home. The next day in school, we hardly spoke. I remained far, far away from him, but noticed that he was always upset.

It truly surprised me that a young man would say anything to me at all because I didn't have nice clothes. In the winter in the seventh grade, I didn't have a warm coat. I wore a vinyl jacket and vinyl in the winter cracks, leaving me very cold.

We were so poor that I was wearing boots that had holes in the bottom, dragging my socks. Before long, there was an awful smell coming from my socks and you could smell it with my shoes. I had to put my socks on the heater so they could dry and that made them hard.

Back in those days, we had heaters on the floor and we would put clothes on them so that they could dry. Once they were dry, we'd wear them the next day.

Our whole neighborhood was struggling and sometimes we'd be fighting among ourselves. Even though we fought, we would come back together.

It was during this time that my hair grew so long and my body became curvy. My legs were shapely from practicing track and running up and down steps around the block.

My mama was not a hairdresser, but I knew how to style hair. She really did the best she could to all of our hair. Sometimes Uncle Louis' wife would curl my hair and the curls would be so tight. They looked nice but so much grease was on my hair.

Whenever I went to my uncle's house, it was always crowded with young and older men. These men were drinking and when my aunt walked out the room, one of them would say things to me like, "Baby you want this quarter? You have to touch me."

I didn't understand any of it at that time, but now I do.

When they touched me, it made me feel some type of way. I could feel myself getting warm. Today, I know those were sexual sensations, and my hormones were aroused. Those moments showed me as a young girl how to use my body.

Making Poor Decisions

For the next couple of years, I made some unusual bad turns.

These were decisions that would affect me later on in my life. I felt out of place at times and worst of all, if a boy said something to me, I responded incorrectly. I didn't know any other way becuase I had never been on dates and had no experience with boys.

If a boy told me to meet him somewhere in the park, or behind the house, I would do it. If he wanted to touch me, I would allow him to do so.

We had a corner store on the same street I lived on and I asked the owner for a job. In my mind, I needed to make a little bit of money to buy myself things like stockings, perfumes, and feminine things girls my age liked.

He said yes, and allowed me to come and work for him. He was older and it gave him a chance to sit down. I would work, but I had sticky fingers.

I put quarters in my socks being young and naive. As I was leaving to go home, you could hear the quarters jingling. I thought I had gotten away, but I really did not.

The owner never confronted me.

My behavior was reckless! When I was stealing, what was my motive? I needed to buy school lunches and other things that I thought were important.

* * *

My brother McKinley had a paper route and to us, his sisters, it seemed like he always had money. We searched his room trying to find his money and we'd spend it being so young.

I did not realize that having a paper route meant he had the responsibility to turn the coins over once he collected the money on a weekly basis. By us taking his money, he lost the route due to never turning the money over on time. Then our life began to change in the house.

Our parents started having family at our home on Friday nights. We played poker, and pokeno with pennies. A lot of the games we played were with cards such as Concentration and War.

In the daytime, especially in the summertime, we would go to the park and play kickball in the yard. The park always had so many activties going on for children. There were jacks contests, ping pong, and merry go round. Most of the time we got chased home from those events in the park. I do not know if it was because we were so small or because we were new to the area.

* * *

I was glad that summer was over because I was entering into eighth grade. I met some amazing girls that school year and we became friends for a very long time.

Sue Smith lived right next door, and my God, she was so talented, and gifted. In those days, everyone was poor, including us. Sue's family looked like they had it better than us, but really they had issues too because Sue's father drank a lot.

Sue was so talented, smart, and beautiful. She knew that her family could not buy clothes for the entire family, due to their jobs and the mill. They were laid off a lot.

Sue became a good seamstress and learned how to make her own clothes, and coats. She was extremely good at making clothes. I liked being around her. She was very sweet, and her spirit was fun, loving, and full of life.

Then there was Brenda.

Whenever my parents allowed me, I would go over her house. I'd start at Brenda's house, then make my way over to Sue's house.

I adored watching her do her hair, she was just special. I could have stayed for a long time at both of their houses because they were clean and homey.

Even if Mrs. Smith was drinking, she would not bother the children on their visits. So we became the Three Musketeers: if you saw one you saw the other two.

We walked eleven blocks to school because there was no bus transportation at the time. As we walked together, Sue and Brenda would talk about their dates the night before. They both had boyfriends and were allowed to date; something I was not permitted to do.

They would beam and laugh about the nice time they had and sometimes they would double date. I was so fascinated to hear about their dating experiences. Not only did they double date, they went skating. I was just happy that I had some friends who liked me for me.

There were mornings Brenda would come by and pick me up first on our way to school. Then we would walk around the block to pick up Sue. I remember one particular morning as I opened the door for Brenda, roaches fell from the frame of the door. Brenda was so kind, she acted like she didn't see the roaches hitting the floor. If she told Sue, it was never mentioned to me and it was never brought up.

When this happened, it took me back to when I was in grade school, around the fifth grade. I brought a roach to school, and it came out of my desk. My school mates made fun of me for years. They gave me a nickname, which was 'Roach Girl.' These girls never teased me and never mentioned it. I knew that I had found some true friends for life.

Remembering My Father...

Daddy was still drinking, and it became heavy. It bothered me a lot to see my dad staggering all the time. But I knew something was wrong because when he wasn't drinking he was with his children, entertaining us.

I honestly looked past all that because I truly loved my dad with all my heart. Daddy was my father, and my hero and he was one in a million. I thank God for a father like him. Being a young father, he could have walked away from his family, but he never thought twice about it.

He was a devout family man who loved his God, mother, wife and his children. Honestly, responsibilities make some black men scared to the point where they throw in the towel, no matter how many children they have. But in the sixties, there were both parents in the home. I believe it made a big difference because both parents shared in the training of the children. In the 1960's, the black family had good and bad times, sunshine, as well as stormy and rainy days.

Most importantly, Daddy was there when we woke up and when we went to sleep. I believed that my dad was special and words cannot express how special my dad was.

I was very upset when I heard my parents having words with one another. As a child, I thought, "How can she be mad at my dad? Or even disappointed?" I could not see it.

But who was I? I was just a child wondering about grown folks business.

I knew my mother would be concerned when my dad was drinking so much, and then go to work. She would be fearful for numerous reasons: he could lose his job or hurt himself on the job.

All my mother wanted him to do was straighten up. Daddy struggled every day walking to and from to work in any kind of weather. He did not want a car. All I Ever Wanted for my daddy was to be a showered with unconditional love.

Nothing more, nothing less.

In times like these, the only thing I knew how to do was pray. Just talk to God; I knew that He would understand. I knew

He would know how I felt even before I asked. I knew that God would make it all right. I knew that He was God, and nothing was too hard for Him.

Casting all your care upon him; for He careth for you.
~I Peter 5:7 (KJV)

I put it in God's hands and wanted my parents to be different. Even as a child, both of my parents had strong family values. Honestly, I am so glad they did.

My dad would get drunk, then came home and lay down. He did not bother anyone. Daddy would struggle up the stairs, get into bed, then sleep until he had to go to work.

I was praying for my father all the time. I would quote **Jeremiah 33:3** which says, *"Call to me and I will answer you and tell you great and unsearchable things you do not know."*

I used to think even when I heard the phone ring it was going to be bad news about my dad. I had many sleepless nights waiting for daddy to come home. Once dad came through the door, I fell asleep.

Daddy was everything to me and there wasn't a doubt in my heart that he loved his family. He was very selfless when it came to his family. He denied himself of so many things to make sure we had what we needed.

And we loved him too.

There wasn't anything that he would not do for my mother and his children. If it was in his power, he would do it. Daddy had good strong legs, but he needed to rest because he walked to work and he worked in the steel mills.

My dad worked three shifts. On pay day, my father would pay his tabs at the bar, and drinking houses where he frequently drank at. We also had a food bill at the corner store.

Dad and my mother would go into their bedroom to discuss their finances. Dad would hand Mom what she needed to take care of the home and children, and there wasn't much left for him; he said that he did not need much.

In my heart, there was not another man like my father. He was so patient and his love was beyond words. It amazed me how much he could witshand. But when he had had enough, everyone knew it. I am like my dad, I can take a lot but when I have had enough, you will know it.

Like I shared, daddy drank and drank, and then my mother would nag him; that was all I remember. Daddy would say, "Please be quiet."

But no, she went on like a broken record. Many times all you'd hear is a door shut, and he was gone. It seemed like he was gone for hours.

Sometimes their argument would be so intense. As a child, when you see your parents arguing, it scares you. In your little mind, you think something bad is going to happen. We as children would hide behind the couch.

I realized that words can hurt, cut down to the soul and you will regret your words later. I wanted to hold my father and let him know that he was the greatest.

Daddy was in a lot of pain and I knew alcohol was the reason why. I knew he used alsohol to hide or drown his feelings. Sometimes I wondered how he kept himself from fighting anyone because he was not a fighter.

We knew not to take sides and go up against my mother because she was strong. She was the disciplinarian when it came to the girls. Daddy would not speak often to the other girls, but with Rhonda, he would. I knew that my parents were survivors, I watched them go through.

Daddy never left, they never separated, slept in separate rooms, or on the couch. When I witnessed all this, it gave me courage and hope.

---

*The obstacles were what they were. Though you may get knocked down, like a boxer in the ring, pick yourself up, **laugh** and try again. Don't give up!*

I heard God say in **II Corinthians 4:8-9**, "*We are hard pressed on every side, but not crushed; perplexed, but not in despair; persecuted, but not abandoned; struck down, but not destroyed.*"

Yes, daddy had struggles as a black man, husband, and father, yet he was happy to be all of those. Mama's family became his

46

family. There was an old saying that he remained broke because he had so many girls and they needed so many things.

Every time he turned around, there was always a need with the family. My dad had a press within him, and I believe to this day, I inherited that from my father. He displayed strength in times of adversity.

There were times when he was not working. Daddy would share about growing up in the south, picking cotton and going to segregated schools. There was one story that I enjoyed hearing about his mother, and grandmother Helen.

Grandmother Helen was a church going, piano playing, religious woman. She didn't drink or smoke and she didn't drive. I believe this was why he didn't mind me going to God's house.

I remember reminding him of his upbringing. I would go to Sunday school and listen to the teaching. But something deep down inside of me would say, "There has to be more than this. Where are the signs, wonders and healings?"

I knew it was the Holy Spirit bringing me to an awareness of my teaching gift.

During this era, it was a man's world and men ran everything. Very seldom would you walk in a church office and see a lot of women. We were unaware there would be a movement in the world like never before.

Once he left home, Daddy stopped going into God's house because his mother took him so much when he was younger. I honestly believe that he had a relationship with God.

The Word of God says, *"Train up a child in the way he should go and when he is old, he will not depart from it."* **(Proverbs 22:6)**

To me, my dad was like a tree planted by the streams of water that yielded it's fruit in his season and its leaf does not wither. **(Psalm 1:1-3)**

Here my dad was, raising two other children who were not his: he stepped up to the plate. What man does that? My dad did. Surprisingly my dad and McKinley had the same birthday.

Won't God do it?

* * *

During this summer of 1969, before entering high school, I had a summer romance with a young man named Alan. I fell hopelessly in love with him.

I met him over a friend's house named Esther Walters. I was always searching for a mother figure, and she filled that space. She lived a block over and she would stop me when I walked by. When we would talk, I found myself sharing my stories and these were things I could not share with my mom.

There were times I would be past my curfew, and I'd run home when the street lights came on. My parents were upset becasue they did not want me in any trouble.

I met Alan at Esther's house, he was staying with her for the summer. We had long talks about why his parents sent him to stay with his aunt, and we became friends.

After our first encounter, I walked around the block to see him. I figured as long as I was in our neighborhood my parents would not mind. I had so many reasons and excuses why I wanted to walk.

I would say things like, "I'm going to the store," or "I am going to the park, I'll be right back."

To be honest, I wanted to see Alan and Ms. Walters. She was so easy to talk to. She made me feel comfortable and did not mind me coming over.

She had children as well: three boys and two girls. The boys were around my age and we recognized one another. Her girls were six, and five years younger than me. I enjoyed doing their hair, and watching TV. It seemed like they had a lot of fun.

After the first time I was late coming home, she made sure that I was home before the streetlights came on.

When I woke up and took care of my household chores, I'd say goodbye and go over to Ms. Walter's house. About the third day after we met, I wanted to braid Alan's hair. He had the biggest afro you ever seen. We went bowling, and it was so romantic.

We would hold hands and walk in the park down the street from where he lived. I was a foolish teenager with a whole lot of immature ideas, like most teenagers do at that age.

I thought we would be together forever. He even carved our names in the tree, not realizing that our romance was just a summer romance.

Memorable moments with Alan where when he would walk over to my house to pick me up. This granted me permission from my mother to leave with him, she adored how respectable he was. Now that I look back, I can really say that I was full of rebellion, although I had integrity.

Alan and I would wrestle in the grass in the park. Wow. He was a perfect gentleman and never tried to touch me, even though I wanted more. If I'd had my way, he would have been the one who I would have sex with in the park; but we didn't.

The next day, when I went over to Ms. Walter's house, he was not there: he was gone. Like the twinkling of an eye, he went back from where he came from. Talking about someone disappointed and hurt. I thought he'd write or come back, but it was as if he was never there.

I never had the chance to say goodbye and that was when I learned about a broken heart. The impact of his leaving was unbearable and my heart was broken into many pieces.

The mind has a way of remembering things. I began to remember the times we shared, and the way he looked at me.

The most important memory was his heartwarming laugh. I had never had so much fun like I had with him. He kept me smiling and laughing; ***I loved to laugh.***

It has been years since I even thought about Alan. As I'm writing at this very moment, I can see his face so clearly. In my mind, I can hear his laughter even though he was gone.

* * *

I continued my relationship with Ms. Esther Walters. She seemed to have a listening ear and it appeared as if she didn't judge me. I just told her what was on my heart because she was my connection to him.

For a long time Ms. Walters would not say anything about Alan. Being so young, I didn't know how to bring up the topic. At that time, if she knew anything, she never volunteered it.

Being a wise woman, maybe she wanted to spare my feelings. By her not mentioning his name, I was finally able to let go of my dreams of him.

Summer have finally ended , so I let go of my dream that he was coming back and went on with my life.

Chapter 2

My High School Years

I was now on my way to high school. If anything, that was frightening because the schools were bigger, with larger halls, new faces, new teachers, bigger goals to reach, and overwhelming dealing with every obstacle in my life.

My mind was determined to laugh at whatever came my way; whether it was good or bad.

I was in the tenth grade when I came down with a serious cough. Later on, I learned it was bronchitis. The cough was so bad that I coughed for a long time in my classes.

My cough sometimes interrupted the class. I took a box of Kleenex to class with me and one of the teachers mentioned that I should stay home. I didn't want to miss school, so I went to school coughing.

School was my outlet and I enjoyed learning. The classes were very interesting, especially history. I perfromed my research at times, and never allowed anyone else to answer.

The teacher gave me a B. He stated that I would have gotten an A, but I talked out of turn in class.

He was right.

I studied very hard and at times, my mother would ease up on being so strict. She allowed me to go to football games after school. The games didn't last long, only from 4:00 to 6:00 PM, and were over before dark.

Finally, I was able to enjoy life like a teenager. Although I enjoyed seeing my classmates, I was a loner who really didn't know how to communicate.

All About Mom...

Allow me to tell you about my mom: she was no joke. If you thought you were getting over on her, think again.

My mom got married while still in high school. She was short and had a lot of hair. Within her family, she was the fourth of seven children. Today, there are two left: my mom and her sister.

My mother woke up fussing and yelling about something; that's all she knew. Maybe that was her way of communicating. She may have been frustrated from having children back to back. There were five: one boy and four girls. So many girls she tried her best to meet our needs. Back in those days, there were times I felt overlooked.

* * *

So much was going on with my sister Rhonda coming and going. But even worse, McKinley started hanging out with boys who stole cars. He and some of his friends stole a car, and found themselves in a wreck. This landed him on probation. He hung out with a particular young man in the neighborhood and they became blood brothers.

Our family was in distress and it was during these times that I needed to be in a place where I could release my frustrations and have hope for tomorrow. It was during these difficult days that I needed to come in from the storms of life to a place of refuge for me; that place was called, 'church.'

Church was the only place I could go to sort out all of my mixed emotions. I had thoughts of suicide and depression plaguing my mind and heart. I had questions that I needed answers to.

When I went to Sunday school, it was not really a full class, just a handful of us. The teacher who was teaching the class did most of the talking, not leaving space for us to ask questions. As a student, I'd listen intensely.

I realized there were some things I didn't agree with. I really didn't know how to express my views without being offensive. I wanted to keep peace, so I sat quietly in my mind.

In my mind, I felt like I sounded stupid. I would not speak up or out, because to me, it was not about who was right or wrong. But I really wanted to ask why weren't any women teaching or preaching?

Something inside of me would say, "I wish I could teach that, I'd teach it a little different if I were given a chance."

But I told myself at the age of seventeen, that they would never receive me. I felt like I'd never be able to speak anything for sure.

I'm glad that I stayed in God's house. I felt like He was faithful in his mercy towards me because I visited the Lord's house on a regular basis. There were times, even as I was growing up, that I should have been dead. But God had his hands on my life.

I used to wonder how I got out of some of the tight spots I had gotten myself into. He was there all the time. Now when I look back, it had to be God. When I open my eyes and realize that I'm still here today, I know that there is a God!

Physicaly, I was maturing and I started to get curves in all the right places. I had a laughing personality and everyone would say, "Debra, you laugh all the time."

Things that were not funny to others were funny to me. Who cared? I just liked to laugh. Especially when it came to TV. I wanted to watch anything that was funny, especially comedy. I've been told by a lot of people that I have laughter in my eyes.

---

* * *

I started taking pride in my hair and the way I dressed. I made a couple of dollars doing chores and would walk to the neighborhood cleaners to get my clothes dry cleaned. I did this with the few clothes that I had and the clothes my aunt gave me. She was slim and dressed like she was young.

I was desperate to be accepted and fit in with the crowd. But no matter what I did, I didn't want people to see me differently from how they used to see me.

It met a girl in my history class named Jill, and we are still friends today. We started talking one day in class about my hair. We later found out she lived a couple of blocks over, so we started walking home from school together. I'd return home and then go back to her house. I had a nice sized afro and she would grease and condition my hair.

As she faithfully took care of my scalp, my hair grew rapidly and became fuller. Through our friendship, we shared lots of stories. I realized that you do not have to wear the latest fashion, and have the baddest hairdos, just as long as your clothes are clean, and pressed.

My dad taught me how to iron clothes when I was seven years old because he wanted his work clothes ironed. My mom hated it, but I was willing to do whatever it took to please him.

Making It Through Highschool...

Entering into my sophomore year of highschool was an accomplishment not just for me, but anyone who lived in the ghetto.

Here I was, running the 440 relay in track, yet I dreamt of taking speech classes in preparation to stand in front of people. I did not know running track was a trick of the enemy.

Speaking in front of people was just where God wanted me. Yes, I shyed away from the class, but deep down inside, I had a feeling in my gut, that I should have took the class. I never let that dream die.

A Good Time Turned Bad...

For once, I was beginning to have a little more freedom. I was able to move around a little more, and took advantage of that. I went over to another friend's house, and her name was Joanne. She was digging a guy from the east side of town.

Back in those days, we would walk to the other side of town like it was nothing. I'd go over her house and we'd end up walking to another side of town, arriving at our destination in no time. We would end up on the east side after laughing, and talking, and not tired at all.

This particular day, we started on a Sunday afternoon. When Joanne and I started out, it was a beautiful day, then we were at her friend's house. I sat in the living room on the couch while Joanne and her friend were in the kitchen. Before we knew it, it got late and we should have left sooner. So she asked one of his male friends to give us a ride home.

She and I had never rode alone in cars before with boys. We did not want to get in trouble, so we accepted the ride since Joanne's friend came along for the ride.

I got in the front seat with the young man who we both knew nothing about. She was alright because she was with her friend in the back. Then all of a sudden both of the young men began talking this funny language back and forth between themselves; they called it Pig Latin. She and I had never heard it before.

As I began listening to them, I got a funny feeling down in the pit of my stomach and I knew something was not right. Then the driver asked us where we both lived and something strange happened.

I was thinking to myself, "Why didn't they drop me off first?" I came to realize that's what they were talking about.

It did not go the way I thought. They dropped Joanne and her friend at her house and left me with this stranger to take me home. I was trying to show him where I lived and what corner to turn on. But like something you see in a movie, he passed it right on by and went a whole different direction. In that moment, I knew I was in trouble.

He took me on a street behind an old abandoned building. I began to look around at my surroundings so I could remember where I was. I noticed railroad tracks nearby. Years later, I looked for that street and I found it.

He parked his car, turned to me, and attempted to touch and kiss me. I began to resist.

Why did I do that?

I kept turning my head every time he tried to kiss me and continued refusing his advances. All I could remember was that he was brave, but his breath smell like balogna. He got so angry with me that he took my left arm and bent it all the way back.

That was so painful.

But I still fought his advances. I was determined that he was not going to do what he set out to do. When I took a look back over my life, now today I realized that it was only the grace of God that I'm still here. I could have have been killed and found later.

As I continued to fight him, and crying at the same time, I believe this scared him. He began to look around to see if anyone noticed us sitting in the car by the railroad tracks. Then out of nowhere a car appeared in sight. It made him so nervous, that right away, he let my arm go and drove me home.

I snuck in the house so grateful and thanking God for coming to my rescue. I was so hurt and wounded. I wanted to tell someone, but who? I took my secret to bed.

I was shaken up so badly inside, realizing how close I came to death. I told myself that I would never forget his voice as long as I lived.

Sleep did not come easy that night. All I could see in my mind was what happened. The pain in my arm was a constant reminder.

I was tossing and turning most of the night. Finally my body relaxed enough to get some sleep. Knowing that I had to get up to face another day, I prayed that everything I was feeling did not show on my face. I was learning how to take all of this to and leave it there.

* * *

The morning finally came and I sought out my friend Joanne at school. I could not wait to tell her what happened. We were in homeroom together, she looked at me and noticed that I was not my happy go lucky self.

She asked me what was wrong and I told her to meet me in the girls bathroom on the second floor. I started telling her about the evening before when she was dropped off safely. Before I knew it, tears were flowing down my face.

She couldn't believe what took place. Her heart was heavy and she felt bad for me. My day was very hard and long and I could not concentrate in my classes. I was in such a daze. It was a bad experience, especially for a young, immature, sheltered young girl. No one should have to go through what I went through.

I learned that some things you cannot share with everyone and I didn't tell Sue or Brenda about it. I did not know if I was ashamed or embarrassed and wanted to keep the whole situation to myself.

Now I know that I should have opened my mouth. Sometimes by releasing and being honest, it could save someone's life. When you go through something, it's not for you, it's for someone else.

I went along trying to put the whole thing behind me. Believe me, it was very difficult. Even my only brother has never twisted his sister's arm that way. As a young woman, you need to be careful. It's a cruel world with cruel people in it. If you think you can trust someone out in the world, and fit in where you don't belong, you will be sadly mistaken. If it don't fit, don't force it.

There is a price you must pay, especially for the foolish and unwise choices you make; there are consequences. What is so foolish is believing as a young teenager that your parents do not want you to have any fun. Enjoy yourself as your parents are required to be responsible for your care and they are watchmen over you.

But when you are so young, you do not understand that concept. The majority of our parents have been places and they are attempting to keep us from walking in their shoes. Today, I can still hear my dad saying, "Daughter you will understand someday; keep living."

Then there will be certain acquaintances they did not allow me be with, yet those were the ones that I was drawn to. We didn't know that they could see things about certain ones that we could not. This is why they are our parents.

After that encounter, Joanne and I did not walk to the east side together again and we never talked about her friend again. If I remember correctly, they did not date much longer after that.

* * *

I believe it was the following week, or a month later that Sue, Brenda and I were walking to school. Sue was upset about her younger sister Pam who was in the hospital. She had been beaten up by a young man who she took a ride from who tried to rape her. When she refused, he snapped on her something terrible!

We continued walking and she mentioned his name.

Something came over me.

When he tried, she ended up saving herself, but gained injuries by jumping out of his car. When we all went to see her, her face and arms were bandaged up.

Man, I felt guilty because I knew I was to blame for not turning him in before all of this happened. Susie's younger sister Pam was full of courage. Thankfully, he got time in jail for the incident.

* * *

Being a sophomore sparked the interest of seniors. They flirted with us, walked us to our clasess, carried our books or whatever it took to get next to us. It seemed like they were rushing or in a contest to see who could be the first one to score with us. As young teenagers, we welcomed the attention everyone gave us. In my mind, I knew it was all a game; they really didn't want us.

There was one young man who kept coming around me who was a quarterback that year. His name was Stan Johns. Every time he came near me, I lit up like a light. I was a square and none of the young boys paid me any attention.

I was amazed.

He asked me to be his girlfriend right away, and I said, "Yes."

By this time, my parents were slightly lifting their ban of strictness. They allowed me to have young boys come over and visit, but they had to leave at a decent hour.

At first, we would see one another at school. I was ashamed of my home because we had roaches and we didn't have nice furniture. He kept asking to come to my house, so one day I allowed him to come over.

I introduced him to my mom and of course, she liked him. We'd sit in the living room watching TV, but my mother was right there standing near the heater on the floor. She was looking, walking back and forth and you could see her peering in the room every time it got silent where we sat.

I honestly thought he really liked me. He played the role to the tee. Mama would love to see him come becuase he was a gentleman and she fell right into his hands. At the beginning, she would not leave the next room and he'd go home at a decent hour.

Then she began to trust us a little more and she went to bed early. That was when he would fondle me and I would allow him. This went on for months until one day I let go, and our hot petting turned into having sex on the couch.

The next day in school, I saw him and we'd smile at one another. But he was not walking with me now. I was confused and hurt because he wasn't communicating anymore. Then it hit me like a ton of bricks: he was after one thing. Now that he got it, he moved on.

I saw him walking with another girl every day. But what I didn't know was that she was holding out because right after graduation they got married. They ended up living on the same block where my parents lived after we moved, and they're still there until this day.

* * *

I continued in my studies and running track, receiving many ribbons but never any trophies.

My family never supported me. When you don't have your family's support, you never know if you were any good. No one cheered me on, but I learned to keep going no matter what.

I finished the rest of the year with my head up although I was ashamed of myself for being silly. Summer was here, so I went to a ball field with one of my girlfriends, not far from my house. She started going with me at first, and we would play basketball.

Once her mom found out that there were a lot of young men there, she told her that she should not go. But I had a little freedom, so I kept going to the field. The guys would tease me and say that I was cocky, whatever that meant. But I played anyway. They played me like they played a dude; I didn't care.

It was at the field that I met Fred Johnson, who was four years older. He would sit on the sidelines watching the whole game, and we played one on one. Sometimes it was for score points up to ten, that way someone else could play.

Fred would always be at the field every time I came. He'd let me miss a shot because I could shoot from the sideline. He commented and sometimes laughed.

I learned to go home before the streetlights came on. One day as I was leaving, he asked me if I was coming back the next day.

I replied, "Yes."

We walked out of the field together because he lived next door to the park and I lived a few blocks away. I thought about Fred when I went home, and when I laid down. I remembered not to be too anxious like I was in my last relationship. But I was happy because someone wanted to spend time with me.

The very next day, I did my chores. When I completed them, I asked my mom if I could go out for a while. I assured her that I would be home before dark.

I started out walking to the field, and once I approached it, I saw Fred on his porch with a couple of his friends. He called out to me to come to where he was on the porch. He was there with his uncle and aunt. I sat there and listened while he explained about his life.

He was home on leave from the military (the Marines). His uncle and aunt had raised him and his two brothers because his mother could not care for him. He never explained why and I did not ask.

After a while, we both went to the field and he was carrying a basketball. We played a couple of games, then sat down on the bleachers as he continued to talk about his struggles. That was when I found out that he was an alcoholic.

He wanted to leave the Marines, and needed my company. He had a lot on his mind and asked me to come back over and eat dinner with his family. He reassured me that they did not mind.

They sat down at the table like a family and began their meal with prayer, like a family is supposed to do. I was so taken aback by the family atmosphere that I began visiting daily. I started braiding his little nieces' hair, who were six and seven.

Sometimes Fred would be in his own world drinking and going in and out of the corner store. His aunt would tell him to slow down and he'd say, "I'm alright."

Sometimes his friends from the Marines would come over to the house and they would be on the porch laughing, drinking and playing music. In his condtion, I knew he could not walk me home. So I would walk by myself before dark.

This behavior went on for months until his leave was up. He took my address, and began to write me from Hawaii. There were times he would even call me from Hawaii. Yes, I would write back sometimes but summer ended in the fall.

My Senior Year In High School

I was going to be a senior in high school, so one day I wrote and told him to forget about me, and find someone who cared about him. I was now enjoying my senior year.

School started and there was a girl in my senior class and we seemed to hit it off. Her name was Roxanne and I walked by her house on my way to school. I never noticed before that she had more privileges in different areas than I did. Her family and her grandmother lived on the corner across the street from one another, and they sold liquor. Surpisingly, she was allowed to drink.

We were in our last year in school and I had to walk by her house to get to the high school. By this time, life was beginning to change. Jill now had a daughter, and Brenda and Sue, were in serious relationships. Even Joanne was doing her thing. That left me and Roxanne to hang out.

I was going on eighteen years old, getting ready to graduate. I felt like everything I went through, no one really cared.

I had stinking thinking.

For all of those times that I didn't get to go anywhere, this was my time and I was finally going to have some real fun. In this era, afros were the hairstyles, and we would pass a store when Roxanne and I walked to school; it was about a block from our high school. This was where we saw guys who hang out in front of the store. They had to have been out of school for maybe two or three years. They'd be drinking singing, smoking cigarettes, and hiding their drinks in a small brown bag.

This was the first time that I was going to try alcohol or whatever we could get; I was so excited! This year was 1972 and they were drinking Boone's Farm, Thunderbird and Mad Dog. We scrambled our little change together and gained enough courage to ask Snake Pipe to purchase our drinks. We asked if he would be so kind as to buy us a pint of Boone's Farm.

Roxane was bolder and had more courage. I came up with this idea that we go to Red Barn, a fast food restaurant right across the street from our high school. We would get drinks, save some of our Boone's Farm inside the drink cups and go back to class.

In those days, we had first, second, and third periods together, and then our lunch breaks. Roxanne and I were in a lot of classes together and we had government in the afternoon.

I wonder if they still have government class today?

We would sit at our desk with our drinks laughing. You know how people act when they are drinking? All the other students would look at us wondering what was was wrong. After laughing histerically, we would sit, be still, and look serious. Then one student told the others that we were drinking. The teacher was older and he didn't know.

Since this was my first time drinking, I got a little tipsy. I ended up spilling my drink, so I went into the bathroom to get paper towels. I made up an excuse and we both left school and went to the store.

The guys were still there, and he bought us another drink. That's what Roxanne and I did the majority of our senior year. When we had general assembly at school, we hung out, drunk drinks, and would sneak into our seats with our drinks. We rolled the bottle all the way down to the front of the assembly, then we'd roll with laughter.

We'd be late going into homeroom in the morning smelling and reeking of wine. That was our specialty. One day, the store was out of Boone's Farm and the Jug, so we had Snake buy us Mad Dog. I had never drunk it before and when I took one sip, it landed me on my behind, and I couldn't get up.

Everyone thought it was funny, but I did not. I didn't want to get in trouble, so I muscled up some strength and staggered down the hall. I felt bad and I told myself I would not drink that again.

We'd ride in her cousin's car drunker than a skunk. My parents never noticed becuse they were drinking too. I'd come home, go straight to bed, then wake up and start all over again.

Losing A Friend...

On a cold wintry night in December of 1972, that evening, I received a call from Roxanne asking me if I wanted to go buy wine. I checked on everyone and they were sleeping so I told her I could come out.

Mom and Dad were out partying, so I snuck out the basement window and walked up to her house. We walked around to the store and Snake was out there by himself that night. He asked us if we wanted to hang out with him.

You know we said, 'yes.'

We were riding with Snake and he was driving and playing music on his eight track, we listented to eight tracks back then. It was getting late, so he drove me home, and Roxanne called me when he dropped her off.

The next day was a Saturday and I was going to sleep in when I received a call from Roxanne. She asked me if I read the newspaper. I told her, 'no.' She told me that after Snake dropped her off, he was killed. His picture was on the front page of the newspaper.

I hung up and read the paper. Sure enough, he had gotten into an argument with someone and they shot him in the head. When I saw the time, it scared me. He dropped me off at eleven, Roxanne right after me and he was killed at twelve.

That shook me up!!

Once again, I escaped death and God had me surrounded by His angels. We were so sad our friend was gone. We used that as an excuse to drink more and became alcoholics after that.

* * *

Everyone knew that we would walk across the stage to receive our diplomas drunk. But I begged to differ.

Then something strange started happening. When I was drinking, I would have pain in my lower abdomen. These were strong, consistent pains. At first, I would not say anything but then the pain would double me over.

We were over Roxanne's house and the pain became unbearable. I got so paralyzed with pain that her parents decided to take me to the hospital.

My parents were called and we learned that my appendix had ruptured. It was removed in the middle of April, and the doctor said I needed six weeks to recover. I'd have to be home schooled, but there was no way I was going for that.

I began to think of a way I could get back to school because I knew that I could not drink if I had to stay home for six weeks. Not only that, I wanted to be with my classmates.

I was at home about four weeks when a classmate named Rocky came to my house. Somehow, he heard of my dilemma and wanted to help. He offered to take me to school and back but my parents had to go to the school and talk to the principal Ms. Love Shepherd.

I was in a wheelchair, but Principal Shepherd saw how much it meant for me to be able to graduate on time with my class. Even though Rocky was bringing my homework to me and the teachers were giving me time to complete everything, it meant more to be in the classroom.

These were the things I expressed to Principal Shepherd. She heard the sincerity of my cry, and to my amazement, offered me the school elevator. The elevator was exclusively for the teachers, but to go to classes, I needed assistance that Rocky couldn't give me.

We had some classes together but not all. So when Principal Shepherd expressed her concerns about a trustworthy person to accompany me, right away, I thought of Roxanne.

Principal Shepard called her to the office out of her classroom over the loudspeaker. Once inside the office, Principal Shepherd offered to instruct us on how to use the elevator. She advised us that when we saw a teacher coming to the elevator, to allow him or her in. I would keep the keys for the six weeks but report back to her in the morning and in the evening.

In the beginning, Roxanne and I did very well. The first three weeks we would get in the elevator, and allow the teachers in when they were standing there and let them off. Then something shifted and the devil got into us as I started to feel better, and got stronger every day.

Then we started being devilish.

When we saw the teachers coming, we'd close the gate and

leave the teacher waiting until we got off the elevator. Then the elevator would go back down.

We would laugh so hard.

We did this until the following week. We thought one of the teachers would report us, but they did not. It was said that whatever you do in the dark will come to the light.

We continued going to class and carried on with the prank. But this time, I was in the fifth week of using the elevator and had become strong. I was now walking without the wheelchair when Rocky would pick me up and drop me off. I would stand in the classroom without the wheelchair, and I'd do this whenever the teacher was facing the blackboard.

My classmates would look at me and laugh saying things like, "Debra, you need to stop!"

I would stand straight up, then turn around; the class would laugh. Then the teacher would turn around, and down I went. Why I did this, I do not know.

School was where I could have fun, and do things to be accepted. I tried to fit in wanting my classmates to like me so I could move past being the girl who brought a roach to school.

I was the girl who did not have pretty clothes, or nice hairstyles. I just wanted to fit in, not realizing that I was not supposed to. I didn't fit in, and it was not going to happen. But I did not understand that at the time.

The year was 1973 and our school, South High School, was hosting our first variety show. I was so excited and I told Roxanne that we should go. There were people who I wanted to see in the show. The show was on a Friday night at 6:00 PM.

Roxanne and I got dressed and we went to the show. As soon as we stepped into school, right at the top of the stairs when you come through the doors, there was Principal Shepherd.

We stopped dead in our tracks.

Now I understood what you do in the dark will come to the light. Principle Shepherd, cool, calm, and collected looked at me and said, "Deborah, I see you are doing really well. No wheelchair and you're running."

Yes, we were running into the school building.

Principal Shepard's next words were, "Deborah come Monday morning return the keys to me. I see you will not be needing them any longer."

Busted, busted!!

At that moment, Roxanne and I knew that it was over. We continued on to the variety show and had a wonderful time. We went home and talked on the phone waiting for Monday.

Monday came and I had a very hard time returning those keys to Principal Shepherd. I didn't want to walk up the stairs like everyone else and there wold be no more pranks on the teachers.

I told myself since this was my last day, "I'm going to enjoy this last day." So, I rode the elevator one last day, but Principal Shepard never called me on the loud speaker. I guess she figured she'll bring the keys by the end of the day.

That's what I did. I brought the keys at the end of the day and put them right in Principal Shepherd's hand. She thanked me and that was the end of that.

Graduation Day

Graduation day arrived and my drinking had slowed down due to the surgery. The day was finally here, June 6, 1973 and the day was special.

To everyone's surprise, I walked across the stage to receive my diploma and I was sober. But afterwards, prom and everything that goes with graduation was worth putting in all of those years. Roxanne and I were now attending graduation practices and I had a drink for myself.

It was so much fun. She and I went to the parties every day for a whole month dancing, and getting stoned. But that's what you do when you graduate.

But what was I going to do with my life???

Chapter 3

My Adulthood Years

Once all of the partying was over, reality set in. What was I going to do now? College was not in my plans and I believe it was because neither of my parents finished school.

I felt scared, lost, and confused.

I never thought about what I was going to do next. Then I had this great idea to join the military, and signed up for the Army. But when it was time for me to go to Cleveland to take the test, I chickened out like a baby. Honestly, once I really thought about it, I knew that I would be home sick. So it was not good for me to go.

In the end, I decided to go to a business college for two years for office machines. Back in those days, computers were not thought about. The class consisted of filing, and the word processor was a typewriter.

Oh, how the world has changed!

I did not want to drink my life away like my father. So I finished college and it was not easy at all. After all the hard work I invested into schooling, I did not want to sit behind a desk. So I went to work doing various jobs such as cashiering, babysitting, and bartendering. Strangest thing was the job I enjoyed most was being a bartender.

I met so many interesting people. I met men and women who would sit at the bar telling me about job openings. But there was a slight problem: I didn't have transportation. I would pay people to take me to places to put in applications.

One day while I was bartending, there were a lot of conversations about the steel mills that were closing down. Men and women were very upset at the possibility of losing their jobs. The majority of them only knew about working in the mills, and had no education.

A lot of those who worked in the mills came up from the south, like my dad. I had been bugging my dad to get me a job in the mill, but he always said the same thing, "No! No daughter of mine will be working in the mills with all of those men who are looking for women."

He wasn't having it.

After a while, I stopped asking because he wasn't budging. Not only that, Daddy never wanted it.

One day, when I was pouring one of the regular customers a drink, he asked me my name. I told him, then he said, "I heard that they were going to hire at GM (General Motors), one of the biggest auto plants in Lordstown.

This was the first time I ever heard about General Motors and what it did. He said, "You should put in an application, you're young."

I was not even twenty one. He continued saying, "You don't need to work in any bars."

I told him, "I don't have any transportation."

That was when he volunteered to take me the next day to complete the application. I took the tips that I received and gave them to him.

Bless the Lord! He took me to General Motors in Lordstown!

That was September 7, 1977. Two weeks later, on September 21, 1977, I received a phone call from The human resources department of GM, asking me to come in that day, bring my ID and do a drug test.

The gentleman who took me before did not hesitate when I asked him to take me again. He reassured me that they were going to hire me, and after the interview, they told me that I was hired. My first production day was October 3, 1977.

For the first six years straight, we worked ten hour shifts for five days a week and eight hour shifts on Saturdays with no layoffs.

I bought my first new car, a 1978 Buick Opel. For the first time, I had charge cards from Livingston's, and JC Penny. I dressed with shoes and matching purses and never missed a beat.

I enjoyed the good life and traveled to places kike Niagara Falls in Canada, to Cleveland Cavaliers games, and a boxing match between Leon Spinks versus Muhammad Ali. In 1978, we saw Don King with all his wild hair, standing on top of his head.

I was able to buy my mom and dad things that they wanted like pool sticks, bedroom dressers and appliances. My dad would drive my new car whenever he was traveling.

You can have all the money in the world and still won't be happy, and I wasn't. I knew that something was missing and there was a void in my life.

I thought to myself, "I need to get back into church. I miss the fellowship of the saints and I missed hearing the Word of God."

Around the age of 25 or 26, I re-dedicated my life back to Jesus Christ because I needed him so badly. I put money and things in front of Him and my life was not fulfilled.

When I turned my life over to Jesus Christ, I had purpose. I had joy, unspeakable joy!!

My Relationship With The Lord...

I got in a gospel choir because I loved to praise the Lord. I began running for Jesus and taking people to the church by witnessing and going to conventions. The bonds I developed with the Christians soldiers lasted until today.

Everything changed about me my personality, but my heart was the biggest change. I became more loving, caring, and giving. I would give you my last if I came by your house and you didn't have food, I'd take you to get food.

There was a time I remember picking up a new convert, and I stopped by her house. I asked her, "Why didn't you call me if you needed a ride?"

She told me, "I didn't have a phone." At that time, cell phones did not exist.

She and I went to a small department store and picked up a

a landline phone for her. I also gave her money to get her phone turned on.

Helping her reminded me of what the Bible tells us to do when we are in a position to help others. We have a responsibility to bless those who have a need. If we don't help, then the love of God does not dwell in us.

If anyone has material possessions and sees a brother or sister in need but has no pity on them, how can the love of God be in that person?

~I John 3:17 (NIV)

Ever sense I can remember, I have always helped people. People told me that people were using me. Now today I know that it's a God given gift.

The Bible says in **I Corinthians 12:27** that God has appointed peope in the church, who can help others. I always helped people in the natural. But when I became spiritual, it seemed like God would put people along my path who needed help.

I am not saying that I had it all together because I still had struggles and one of my struggles was sex. Not saying that I gave myself to every man who I dated or was involved with, because I did not.

But there were times that I was weak, giving into temptation. And when I did, I would feel so bad afterwards. Yes, I would repent being a born again Christian because this made a big difference in my life.

When it came to making decisions, I would pray and allow the Holy Spirit to give me the answer. I made sure my decisions lined up with the word of God. Even though I was involved in church doing what I needed to please the Lord, my desire changed about General Motors.

The more I grew closer to God, I began questioning myself, "What was I doing at General Motors? Why was I still there?"

It got to the point that I dreaded going to work and the money didn't matter anymore. I had been there for ten and a half years and every time I stepped into General Motors, I did not have peace. My Peace was gone and I wasn't happy.

God was dealing with me when General Motors began offering buyouts to pay for years employees were there. I believe I heard God's voice, but fear gripped me.

I didn't act on it.

It was 1988 and so many rumors were circulating around the plant and the assembly workers were saying the plant was going to shut down and relocate. Some of my co-workers relocated to different plants in various other cities such as Kansas City, and Flint Michigan.

At first, I did not know if I heard from God so I didn't go to the main office and sign up for the buyout. But when it came and left, I knew that I should have signed up. I had an uneasy feeling about it. And I was walking around the plant thinking, "I missed God."

Many other workers who took the buyout were born again believers. The majority of them belonged to the same church.

I attended New Fellowship Pentecostal Church in Youngstown, Ohio.

It really did not have anything to do with what church you belonged tp. It was all about knowing God as your source. Everything you need and everything you have, comes to you through Him. He is the source and my faith was not there.

I could believe Him for a car, house, or even a job. But to leave a job that took care of **all** my needs, it took trusting God and I hadn't developed that type of trust. My confidence was not in God, and you are talking about being miserable. When you do not obey God, you will literally be miserable. Words cannot really explain when you do not obey God. All I know is you will have no rest.

Praying For A Shift

I continued working there, but I was in a daze every day. I was upset with myself because I was still at a job where I did not want to be. Please do not get me wrong, I'm grateful for General Motors because they were good to me. Even until today.

I was truly blessed to work for a company that had so many benefits. Even after ten years at the company, You can get your pension when the time is right.

When I disobeyed God, I had so many accidents after that. I almost got ran over by a tow mower in the plant by walking between two aisles. I was not focused, not alert, nor paying attention due to my decision a year prior. I came to work and didn't want to communicate with anyone.

I spent most of my time reading my Bible and praying. Yes, I prayed on my way to work and on the job, I just prayed. I needed to hear from God.

In the meantime, I went back to school and attended Gordon James Career Center for Medical Assistant. I just wanted out of that place because so much was going on inside the plant. When you work in that type of environment, you see so much and you learn to stay away from certain people because of what they were doing.

I continued serving God to the best of my ability. But I lacked confidence when it came to leadership, so I stayed in the background.

Finally, someone came up to me and asked me if I heard they were doing the buyout again. It was around October or November of 1988, and I was now a young thirty three year old. I knew deep down in my soul that the Holy Spirit gave me another opportunity to make it right.

Everybody was talking about the buy out and how much they were offering. They were giving people time, but there was a deadline. It was already October and the buyout was over November 30th.

I was seeking God like never before, praying, fasting and asking the Lord to speak to me. I needed to hear from Him. I was now at the point in my life where I was finally ready to leave, knowing that the Lord was my source. Everything that I needed, He would provide.

I continued to work and the buy out was in my mind daily. I

kept what I was thinking to myself, when deep down inside, I knew what I had to do. But I had to find the right time.

I started thinking really hard about the decision that I was going to make. I had to consider not having the income every week.

It was a faith walk.

I was also concerned about losing my benefits and had so much to consider when I made this life changing decision. All I knew was I had spent eleven and a half years at a place that I was now over with. I dreaded getting up going to work. It was great working long hours and making long money. But as I grew up, money did not mean that much anymore: I just wanted out.

Pursuing The Buyout

I began inquiring about the buyout. I took a step of faith and went to the human resources office to set up an appointment to discuss it. I wanted to know all about it.

People stopped by and asked me if I was seeking the buyout, and I was not going to lie, so I said, "Yes, I am thinking about it."

People were trying to discourage me by saying things like, "You do not have a husband. You're going to lose your benefits. What are you going to do?"

I heard everything everyone said, but my decision was made. It was time for me to go back to human resources to set up another appointment. It ended up being the following week.

I decided to let my parents know my decision. I went to their house, sat down and let them know that I was going to leave General Motors after eleven and a half years.

I explained to them that I was not happy. My mom didn't understand but my daddy did because he took an early retirement when the mill shut down. All he said was, "Daughter, I am with you if that is what you want to do."

I understood when my dad said that it did not matter what anyone else said at General Motors. I went to work and stayed to myself. When people came to voice their opinions, I didn't even hear them. I put my earplugs in my ears and covered my hair.

The day came: November 9, 1988. This was the day for me to go into the human resources and sign the papers that released me from General Motors. They let me know that yes, I may lose my benefits. But when I turned fifty-five or sixty-two, I was entitled to a pension since I had put in ten years under the old plan.

This remained in my memory.

* * *

When I turned fifty-five years old, I called General Motors and asked about my pension. They advised me that I should wait until I turned sixty-two because I would get more. I was in a place that I needed it.

* * *

So I signed all the necessary papers and left human resources

When I came out of the office, co-workers were standing around. I would say about ten to fifteen people were waiting to see if I was going to go through with what I was saying for the past month.

Standing there and spying on me didn't make a difference to me at that present moment. I made my decision and was at peace. It was as if I didn't see them, and I instantly came out leaping straight up in the air full of unspeakable joy.

Words cannot explain. I kept walking past all of the spectators and they were still on my heels. That day was my last day.

Glory to God!

God blessed me with a gracious check for all the years I gave to General Motors and I was finally at peace. I was young when I started working for them at twenty-one years old, and now here I am thirty-three years old and I did not know what lied ahead. But that door was closed.

I can honestly say that I never regreted the decision. First thing I did was gave an offering to the Lord. Yes, I paid my tithes and offering. Then I took care of some of my old bills, paid off debts and I had some leftover.

This was the time for me to begin a new chapter in my life. For sixty days or so, I just relaxed, cleaned my house and took care of my parents.

People, mostly Christians, saw me pull up in a new car. I was loaning money to everyone. Some paid me back and still to this day, some have not. But God has always blessed me.

I never said that I'd never work again, I just did not want to work in a plant. Being out of work for a while, I made another decision. I considered, "What if my car breaks down? I'm going to need finances to fix it."

A sister in Christ came to me and asked me if I would consider taking care of people in a nursing home? I said yes, because I enjoyed doing that.

My sister in Christ, Lynn got me a job at a long term care facility as a private duty caregiver. Back then, they were beginning classes to Be an STNA (State Tested Nursing Assistant), and without license, a CNA. My sister in Christ whose name was Sarah talked to her supervisor explaining my situation. She gave me a job for the first time where I took care of someone inside of a facility.

I worked five days a week from 9:00 to 1:00 PM providing care for an elderly man. I washed and dressed him. At first he did not want me to care for him because of my skin color. It took some time adjusting on both sides. He was not really happy to see me some days and he grumbled at me. This indeed was different from working on cars.

Now I was doing what I did best, which was taking care of people, and helping someone who needed me. I didn't allow his attitude to affect what I needed to do for him. He needed me to assist him and I really wanted to, no matter how he felt.

Once he got used to me, he didn't want anyone else to take care of him. I was alright with that so I took care of him.

Six months later, he passed away.

By that time a class was instituted at the nursing home and I took it. I passed the entire test so I could become a state tested nurses assistant (STNA). I made a little more money, and I had more responsibilities as an STNA, and more patients to care for.

I had developed a routine and all of the patients loved me. I took time with them to comb their hair, and I dressed them well. I gave them the best care they deserved.

The state came in and said we were only allowed to have ten patients per worker. I went to work every day and picked up extra shifts when I could. I enjoyed taking care of the sick, shut in, and elderly.

I remembered that I had parents too, and my patients could be my parents. For this reason, I treated them like I would have treated my parents and it became natural for me.

* * *

After I had been on the job for six months, I wanted to switch to the night shift. I waited until until an opening came up and when it did, to the night shift I went.

Night turn was better for me because I could get so much done during the day. I had time to do what I needed to do and I took advantage of that.

While I was enjoying my newfound career, I began to notice a change in my father.

Chapter 4

Losing My Father

I had been on the job approximately three years, when I noticed my dad was changing.

I couldn't put my finger on it, but his behavior was different. He stopped going over his family's house to play cards on the weekends and he was always sitting in his chair in the living room.

He used to get up and greet me when I walked in the room, but he was no longer doing that. This caused me to question if my dad was okay. I would ask him if he was ok, and he always answered, "Yes."

But my father was no longer the man that I was used to seeing. I was accustomed to my fahter being a strong, moving, talkative man, whenever I walked through my parents door. Now when I walked through the door, my dad would be sitting in his chair and I would walk up to him and plant a kiss on his forehead.

We would engage in conversation, and he'd be walking and talking to me and moving around. I left, and I would come back a couple of days later, to find my dad still in the same spot in his chair, working puzzles. I began joking with him as I usually did and played in his curly hair.

I can still hear him saying, "Stop that daughter."

I would say, "Oh Daddy that's not hurting you." I always played in my dad's hair.

On this particular visit, I said, "Daddy let's walk to the door."

He said, "Daughter, I'm tired. I do not feel like moving."

It was at that moment that I asked my mother when was the last time that daddy had been to the doctor because he was not acting like himself. My mom reassured me that he had an appointment at the end of the month. I said that I would go to his appointment with them.

My dad knew how I was and I was disturbed about my dad's condition. He became smaller than last time I saw him, but I never voiced it.

I said to myself, "I wonder what is really going on? Were they keeping a secret from us?"

I continued on with my life, checking on my dad daily. Then the day came when my sister and mother had to take daddy to the doctor. I was waiting patiently for whatever was wrong with my dad. I kept calling my mother's cell phone and no one would answer. When they finally did, the news was grave.

The Diagnosis

They admitted my dad and right away, he was diagnosed with prostate cancer. I ran up to the hospital as fast as I could get there. They gave my dad until Christmas to live because his cancer was spreading rapidly. I cried out to my God asking Him to give my dad time. I pleaded with the Lord, "Please don't take him before Christmas!"

I was not ready to let my father go and I was not prepared for the news that I received at that moment. I literally stopped living and lost focus on matters concerning me because I could not imagine my life without my dad. I was scared, so I went to the church and asked them to put my dad on the prayer list.

I was in a daze, and I couldn't think or sleep. My mother was also hurting, but we didn't know how to comfort her because we all were in pain ourselves.

The doctors advised our family that daddy needed surgery right away. We had a conference call and came into agreement. When the surgery was over, we all were waiting for Daddy to come out but we had to wait until the doctors received the results of all the tests.

* * *

Glory to God, My dad made it until Christmas. God answered our prayers and we were so overjoyed!!

* * *

We never left Daddy's side.

I worked midnights and when I got off, I went straight there so he knew he was not alone, and he was loved. He would talk to us as much as he could, which was not a lot.

This was the first time that my dad was ever operated on and he was in a lot of pain. He was trying to hide it, but I knew my dad was suffering. It was all over his face: such sadness.

The doctors wanted to send daddy to a nursing home straight from the hospital for rehabilitation for thirty days. The rehabilitation was so he could walk again and get the care he needed.

We as a family approved and rallied around my dad, giving him all the love and support he needed. Once he was there, we were there everyday and faithfully made sure that he was getting the quality care he needed.

Dad tried his hardest to entertain us, but he could not bounce back. Then the doctor ordered more tests and said he found more cancer and it had spread throughout his body.

Daddy pleaded with me not to allow them to operate on him again, so I reassured him that they would not once his thirty-day rehab was over. We made plans to bring him home but he was not strong enough to walk the steps at the house.

We all decided to make eveything comfortable for him, so mom put a hospital bed in the living room. That's where we all spent our last days with daddy.

He was in so much pain as the cancer ripped through him, leaving him frail and shallow. Some days, I stayed away because I couldn't face my dad wasting away. The more I went over to the family house, the more I left feeling deeply depressed. All I could do was smoke marijuana regularly; it became my way of escape.

Mom told us that Daddy would scream at night begging for more pain medicine. She had to be strong for them both as his days got shorter. I do not know how my mother did it. How did she have the grace to watch the man who she was married to for years fade away?

* * *

One day, it was just my dad and I. I asked him if he knew Jesus, and to my surprise, he told me that he made peace with God and he had surrendered. I was so elated because I wanted to see my dad when I got home. From that point, we began putting his homegoing celebration together.

I did not want to think about Daddy. He began to sleep more and I could see him slipping away. It was in the winter time and Christmas came and went. Now it was almost February 13, 1999, Daddy's birthday. He was so worried and happy that his birthday was coming and all he wanted was to live to see his birthday.

Daddy's birthday finally came and Daddy was extremely happy. We all gathered around him and sang, "Happy birthday." He made it to see sixty six years old and we all were happy for him.

Daddy was fine for a couple of days, then all of a sudden, his personality began to change. He began to drift away and I could not take it. The man who I adored, and admired was going to leave and there was nothing that I could do. I stayed away and started smoking more marijuana than ever before.

February came and went. March came in and Daddy was slowly slipping in and out. We all continued taking vigil beside his bed daily.

The week of March twenty-second through the twenty ninth, Daddy took a turn for the worse. When my mother became aware, she called us all to be with daddy for his last moments.

Then on March 24, 1999, I came by that morning to sit with my daddy; but he was gone. Mom left daddy there so we all could say goodbye before she called the funeral home.

We all cried and cried.

I was so messed up over his passing. Mom never cried even though he was in a better place and no longer suffering.

This is when my life took a downward spiral.

Chapter 5

My Life Was Out Of Control

I left the family house and went to buy some marijuana, but they were out. They were supposed to get their supply in after my father's funeral, but when I returned, they were still out.

I really needed to get high.

The doorman said, "I got something you may like."

That was when he handed me a crack pipe. I had just got paid and I spent my whole check there like a fish out of water.

I didn't even know how to go about smoking, 'crack.' I didn't even know how to light the pipe, and everyone was stealing my stuff.

I stayed away crying daily becuase I missed my father. I was in so much pain that I went right back over there. The next day, I spent all of my savings that I had put away at home. I did not know what was on me.

The door man later told me that is was called, 'crack cocaine.' It was the first time I had ever heard of it because I had been sheltered all of my life. There I was at the tender age of fourty-four, and a full blown addict. I did not understand the disease of addiction at all and I did everything the disease told me to do.

I was powerless.

I was dealing with a demon and found myself lying, manipulating, stealing things and even sold myself for just one more hit. I went to bed on a mission and I woke up on a mission. I lost my self-esteem, self-worth and my dignity.

Everything was gone.

Before long, I began isolating myself from everyone who was dear to me. I felt so worthless, and ugly on the inside as well as the outside. I felt guilty of how much money I was spending. I was spending my grocery money, rent money, and utility money.

Everything went up in smoke.

All of this took place within six months after my father passed; my life went into a tailspin. I did not care about anything, not even myself. By the end of October 1999, I had had enough, but my addiction lasted nineteen years, until October 12, 2018.

My Road To Recovery...

Someone told me about a treatment center called Pathways Sober House. Even the name itself has a lot of meaning.

This was a place for you to get back on the right path. God bless the awesome, late Apostle Loretta J. Pernice, who had a passion, and her call was to help people with addictions. Whether it was drugs, alcohol, pills, sex, or bad spending habits. She understood all of it being there herself in her earlier days.

The first thing she did was give you a place to stay, fed you and clothed you. She taught women how to be mothers, fathers how to be fathers, husbands how to be husbands, and wives how to be wives. She put families back together with their children by hosting parenting classes, and so much more.

When you indulge in addiction, you lose all your principles, morals, and upbringing. Besides all of that, she gave everyone who came through the doors salvation. You were introduced to Jesus Christ.

Many of us have walked away from God. The drugs became our God so we had to be taught about our Savior.

We came to a place of gratitude, because we could have lost our lives in those streets. But God had his hands on us. She explained to us that we needed a power greater than ourselves, and we chose that power to be Jesus Christ.

I liked being there.

I was the only one from Youngstown at that time. Everyone else was from Warren, Ohio.

* * *

Once I was off restriction, I received a job in a nursing home called New Day Skill Center in Warren, Ohio. Someone would take me and pick me up.

Pathways Sober House was at the old St. Joseph Hospital in Warren. It was Apostle Pernice's vision to start a church, and the Lord instructed her to knock down the walls in the lower basement and start the church.

At the treatment center, we started every day at 8:00 AM to 4:00 PM knocking the walls down. Still to this day, Elim

Christian Center is established, but the church moved to a bigger building on Ridge Road in Warren, Ohio.

We had prayer every morning, classes, Bible study and yes church. I relapsed a couple of times, left and came back.

Chapter 6

The Diagnosis

I was working day turn at the nursing home from 6:00 AM until 2:00 PM. At this time, it was now November of 2004 and I really wasn't paying attention to my body.

I thought it was the job because I began to feel tired all of the time. Sometimes I was weak, dizzy, warm and sweating at night. When we had classes and even bible study at church, I would fall asleep.

I could not stay awake.

I made the assumption that it was work and church because sometimes we would be at church late. But when I went to work, it took me a longer time to get my patients up. I still never thought any more about it.

I was always short of breath, tired and couldn't understand why. I'd always snack at night but when I woke up in the morning, the snack would be still there. I just figured that I went to sleep.

This happened more than one time in a week. I would come home from work taking a nap. I'd never been a person who took naps, and someone would have to come and knock on my door to get me to come to dinner. I would not make it and I wasn't hungry.

I noticed that I was also losing weight and my hair was falling out. All of this finally got my attention and I took notice of all the changes that were going on with my body.

Then on December 3, 2003 while lifting a patient with another aid, my back went out. I had to leave the job and go straight to the emergency room where they gave me a shot in my back. For years I struggled with spasms. It has gotten better over the years, I just cannot bend down like I used to.

Shortly after, my family doctor diagnosed me with asthma, and COPD. All I thought was, "Lord what else?"

I had to do some adjustments behind these conditions, but something more was going on with me. So I began to cry out to God earnestly asking him what was wrong. When I asked the Holy Spirit this question I heard as clear as day, "It's HIV, but it's not until death."

My mind went back to remembrance when I read the Rock Hudson life story years earlier about him contracting HIV.

At that treatment facility, I became close to a young lady named Judy Daly and our friendship exists even until this day. We talked mostly every day and I confided in her what the Holy Spirit spoke to me while I was praying.

I told her that I needed to make an appointment with Planned Parenthood. I made the appointment, and it was for the following week.

* * *

I continued with my daily duties, but now I was getting sicker and losing more weight. At this time, I was already struggling with two ailments.

My back was in such terrible condition that I had to get therapy from a chiropractor three times a week. Then I had to get inhalers, a breathing machine, and my whole life changed.

Here I was, a strong independent black woman, who for the first time in my life had to have people at the facility help me. I was experiencing challenges in so many areas, especially walking to and from the table, and even to drive my car.

Receiving The News...

The time came for me to go to my appointment. December 13, 2004 I took the test and my friend Judy was with me. They said it would take a week for the results and they would call me back no later than a week's time.

But in this meantime, I was very weak. I can remember when I attempted to eat, and my stomach would be so nauseated. I just wanted to vomit but I couldn't.

I stopped working as a nurse's aide because my back did not improve. I had a worker's comp case and was on light duty. My case finally settled a year later because I was broke and had no other income.

After a week passed, I told Judy that Planned Parenthood told me they would call in a week and they didn't. I suggested to her I knew that I had HIV and we needed to go there.

I took off work and then December 20, 2003, we went. I told them who I was and they asked me to sit down and they would call me in the back. When they called me in the back, I already knew.

When I got inside the room, there was a nurse, psychiatrist, and a psychologist all in white smocks watching me as I came through the door. I can still remember it as if it was yesterday.

I said to them, "I already know what I have, please just tell me how or what I need to do to get well." I continued, "I am not going to commit suicide."

Someone called for me to sit down and began explaining to me that I had contracted HIV and that I was very ill. They gave me the name of a doctor who was a specialist in HIV and told me I needed to call them right away. I left there and I made the appointment, which was not until after I talked to the CDC (Centers for Disease Control).

It was a process.

The CDC called me and asked me to come in to talk. This was somewhere in January of 2004. I went to their office and they wanted to know who I believed that I contracted the virus from. I gave them the name and they gave me pamphlets to read as I waited to see the doctor.

My appointment was not until April of 2004. She told me important factors that I needed to know so that I can begin preparing myself mentally.

They advised me that some of the medicine was going to make me sick until my system got accustomed to it. I read all of the pamphlets because I wanted to educate myself.

This was a lot to take in. Here I was at forty-eight years old and had three compromised illnesses; all at the same time. Everything had to change. I needed to eat a lot of vegetables like leafy greens, spinach and food with proteins, so I could had something to fight the disease.

I needed to eat differently as it was right before my April 2004 appointment. After all those months, now I was sick, very sick, and had to be admitted for a blood transfusion because my iron count was so low. I had to get three blood transfusions then I was able to go home that afternoon.

When I got home from the hospital, they wanted to know how did I know that I had HIV. I simply told them that the Holy Spirit told me when I was praying.

Everyone was extremely good to me at the facility.

I had to learn to live with this diagnosis, and my new normal.

Chapter 7

Living, Thriving and Laughing With God

It may have been possibly one or two people who had fear when they were around me. The Bible tells us that our people are destroyed for the lack of knowledge.

My people are destroyed for lack of knowledge: because thou hast rejected knowledge, I will also reject thee, that thou shalt be no priest to me: seeing thou hast forgotten the law of thy God, I will also forget thy children.

~Hosea 4:6 (KJV)

Sometimes when you don't know, you don't know. Those were the moments when I had to share. You can't catch it by touching me and I truly understood their plight and fear.

My appointment came in July and I finally went to the clinic in Youngstown Ohio. My very first viral was April 6, 2004 and it was 518, 018 which was bad and my CD4 was 234. If my reading dropped to 200, I would have contracted AIDS.

But God's hand was on me today and my VL< 20 below 20, CD4 1305 and undetectable.

Praise God!! Nobody but Jesus!!

Now everything was beginning to make a lot of sense. I understood why I had no appetite, weight loss, night sweats, and changing of my skin tones, all that came with it and more. All I knew was that I wanted to live and not die.

Years before, HIV/AIDS was a death sentence. Over the years the medicine have proven to be more effective, and you can live a long successful life with HIV.

I am a living witness.

I can remember when my sister Rhonda passed away and we all went to view her body. When we got there, we all introduced ourselves. The funeral director told us that they were getting calls asking her if it was me, Debra Decembly. I told her when they called again tell them that I'm still standing!!

* * *

I thank God for my friend Judy. She went to every appointment with me, kept me encouraged, and held my hand. Then one day as we left the clinic, she said, "Sis, if you want to cry, cry."

And I did.

I asked the Lord, "Why me?"

His answer was, "Why *not* you? This is not for you. This is for someone coming after you. Someone needs to know how you went through without losing your mind. It's not about you, it's all about Jesus."

Today, all I can say is that it was God who kept me no matter what. When I expressed how I truly felt, I always laughed. When I was going through leadership classes, I sat down and my body was so weak.

I can remember one sister in the evangelistic class said to me,

"Debra God will heal you as you go."

I didn't understand it at that time, but God made a believer out of me. Yes, he is a healer.

As He began to heal my body, everything was funny. I laughed all the time.

I was so grateful that when this happened, I was in a place full of people who cared about me. When I couldn't walk to the dining room to eat, a sister carried me on her back. This was the same person who was fearful to be around me.

Won't He do it?!?!?

* * *

I started out taking my medicine as prescribed. Then I went through periods where I just took it when I wanted to, which wasn't good at all. By me not being consistent, my medicine had to be changed three times. Finally, I was on a schedule where I took it every morning and did not miss a day.

I have been undetectable for *years*, Praise God!!

My Message of Hope

I wrote this book to encourage those who have struggled with and live with HIV. You can do all things that you used to do in God's time.

You will love again! But most of all, love yourself, live your life, have fun, and don't forget to LAUGH!!

I came to a point in my life where I understood that God knows what He is doing. He makes no mistake.

God allowed me to go on this journey to let others know that there was a purpose for my life. Like myself, you'll be able to say, "Lord, I give you the glory!!"

Trust God in your process. He'll see you through because He loves you, and so do I!!!

Live.

Love.

LAUGH!!

About The Author

Debra A. Decembly is a licensed minister, a Certified Peer Recovery Supporter, and a preliminary chemical dependence counselor assistant (CDCA).

Her desire is to be a role model for individuals who have experienced trauma in life, giving them hope that they too can survive through laugher.

Find Debra online:
WWW.DebraDecembly.Com

Follow her on social media:

 **@Debra.Decembly-52**

Other ~Books ~By The Author

Debra compiled this journal to give you space
to write and heal.

It was through her journey of healing and recovery that
she found her solace and peace in writing.

So go ahead, grab your pen, and write yourself
into unspeakable joy!!

Available at
amazon.com

www.ingramcontent.com/pod-product-compliance
Lightning Source LLC
Chambersburg PA
CBHW071015120626
46546CB00003B/1092